CHURCH AND SOCIETY
Advocating for peace and justice

*By Lee Ranck and Shanta Bryant
For the General Board of
Church and Society*

CHURCH AND SOCIETY

Copyright © 2004 by Cokesbury

All rights reserved.
United Methodist churches and other official United Methodist bodies may reproduce up to 500 words from this publication, provided the following notice appears with the excerpted material: From *Church and Society: 2005–2008*. Copyright © 2004 by Cokesbury. Used by permission.

Requests for quotations exceeding 500 words should be addressed to Permissions Office, Abingdon Press, P.O. Box 801, 201 Eighth Avenue South, Nashville, TN 37202-0801 or permissions@abingdonpress.com.

This book is printed on acid-free paper.

ISBN 0-687-00150-1

All Scripture quotations unless noted otherwise are taken from the *New Revised Standard Version of the Bible,* copyright 1989, by the Division of Christian Education of the National Council of the Churches of Christ in the United States of America. Used by permission. All rights reserved.

MANUFACTURED IN THE UNITED STATES OF AMERICA

CONTENTS

Our Identity, Call, and Mission **4**

Acting for Peace and Justice Through the Ministry of Church and Society Work **6**
    From *The Book of Discipline*

Key Tasks to Consider **7**

Four Types of Congregational Involvement **8**
    Social Service
    Social Education
    Social Witness
    Social Action
    Carrying Out a Comprehensive Ministry
    Jesus Got Into Trouble

Leadership Hints **11**

Foundations for Social Involvement **12**
    Scripture
    Tradition
    Reason
    Experience

Getting Started **16**

Cultivating Relationships **20**
    Within Your Congregation
    Within The United Methodist Connection
    Coalitions
    Ecumenical and Interfaith Groups
    Ministry With Those Who Are Marginalized

Checklist for Planning and Action **24**
    Consider Issues/Needs
    Develop Strategies
    Get Approval, Act, Review

Resources **26**

General Agency Contacts .... **Inside Back Cover**

Our Identity, Call, and Mission

You are so important to the life of the Christian church! You have consented to be among a great and long line of people who have shared the faith and led others in the work of Jesus Christ. We have the church only because over the millennia people like you have caught the vision of God's kingdom and have claimed a place in the faith community to extend God's love to others. You have been called and have committed your unique passions, gifts, and abilities in a position of leadership, and this guide will help you understand some of the elements of that ministry and how it fits within the mission of your church and of The United Methodist Church.

"The mission of the Church is to make disciples of Jesus Christ. Local churches provide the most significant arena through which disciple-making occurs" (*The Book of Discipline of The United Methodist Church, 2004*, ¶120). The church is not only local but also global, and it is for everyone. Our church has an organizational structure through which we work, but it is a living organism as well. Each person is called to ministry by virtue of his or her baptism, and that ministry takes place in all aspects of daily life, not just within the walls of the church. Our *Book of Discipline* describes our mission to proclaim the gospel and to welcome people into the body of Christ, to lead people to a commitment to God through Jesus Christ, to nurture them in Christian living by various means of grace, and to send them into the world as agents of Jesus Christ (¶121). Thus, through you—and many other Christians—this very relational mission continues. (The *Discipline* explains the ministry of all Christians and the essence of servant ministry and leadership in ¶¶125–137.)

Essential Leadership Functions

Five functions of leadership are essential to strengthen and support the ministry of the church: identifying and supporting leaders as spiritual leaders, discovering current reality, naming shared vision, developing action plans, and monitoring the journey. This Guideline will help you identify these elements and set a course for ministry.

Lead in the Spirit

Each leader is a spiritual leader and has the opportunity to model spiritual maturity and discipline. John Wesley referred to the disciplines that cultivate a relationship with God as the "means of grace" and suggested several means: prayer, Bible study, fasting, public and private worship, Christian conversation, and acts of mercy. Local church leaders are strongly encouraged to identify their own spiritual practices, cultivate new ones as they grow in their own faith, and model and encourage these practices among their ministry team participants.

Discover Current Reality

"The way things are" is your current reality. How you organize, who does what, how bills get paid and plans get made are all building blocks of your current reality. Spend time with people who have been in this ministry and with your committee members to assess their view of how things are. Use "Christian conversation," one of the means of grace, not only to talk to others openly about their understanding of current reality but also to listen for the voice of God regarding your area of ministry.

Name Shared Vision

"The way things are" is only a prelude to "the way you want things to be." When the church is truly of God, it is the way God would envision it to be. Spend time with your committee and with other leaders in the church to discern the best and most faithful future you can imagine. How can you together identify your role and place in a faithful community that extends itself in its fourfold mission of reaching out and receiving people in the name of God, relating people to God, nurturing them in Christ and Christian living, and sending them forth as ministers into the world? Examine your committee's role and its place in that big picture and try to see yourselves as God's agents of grace and love.

Develop Action Plans

How do you get from here (your current reality) to there (your shared vision)? As a leader, one of your tasks is to hold in view both what is and what is hoped for so that you can build bridges to the future. These bridges are the interim goals and the action plans needed to accomplish the goals that will make your vision a reality. Remember that God may open up many (or different) avenues to that future, so be flexible and open to setting new goals and accepting new challenges. Action plans that describe how to meet interim goals should be specific, measurable, and attainable. While it is faithful to allow for the wondrous work of God in setting out bold plans, balance that boldness with realism. You and your committee will find information and tips here on developing and implementing the shared vision, the goals toward that vision, and the specific action plans that will accomplish the goals.

Monitor the Journey

A fifth responsibility of leaders is to keep an eye on how things are going. Setbacks will surely occur, but effective leaders keep moving toward their envisioned future. Not only will you monitor the progress of your committee's action plans to a faithful future but you will also be called to evaluate them in light of the ministry of the rest of the church. Immerse yourself and your plans in God's love and care. Voices from the congregation (both pro and con) may be the nudging of God to shift direction, rethink or plan, or move ahead boldly and without fear. Faithful leaders are attentive to the discernment of the congregation and to the heart of God in fulfilling the mission of the church.

Acting for Peace and Justice Through the Ministry of Church and Society Work

You are the leader of your church's involvement in social issues. As the ministry team chairperson of Church and Society in your congregation, your first responsibility will be to help your church members respond to pressing social issues by:

- keeping yourself, members of your ministry team, your pastor, and the church council aware of study and action needs and opportunities related to community, state, national, and international issues;
- educating the members of your congregation about those issues (a process often called "consciousness raising"), using study groups, guest speakers, video programs, newsletter articles, Sunday bulletin inserts, field trips, and other educational techniques;
- making connections outside the church and with the church at all levels, with particular emphasis on issues that affect your own community;
- advocating for and responding to the needs of all people in God's world.

From *The Book of Discipline*

The Book of Discipline—United Methodism's book of law—spells out what your congregation can expect from you. Get a copy from your pastor and read the Social Principles and the sections related to your work as Church and Society chairpersons. *The Discipline* ¶ 254 suggests that you keep your church council aware of the needs for study and action on a variety of issues; recommend to the church council social concerns study and/or action projects; cooperate with other ministry teams in your congregation to survey the needs of the local community and to make program recommendations that will help your church respond to local, community, state, national, and international needs; and stay in contact with district, conference, and general church groups working on social issues and providing action suggestions and educational resources.

Besides studying the Social Principles, carefully read ¶217–221 of *The Book of Discipline* on "The Meaning of Membership." Make ¶221 the watchword of your team's ministry: "Each member of The United Methodist Church is to be a servant of Christ on mission in the local and worldwide community."

Key Tasks to Consider

Your personal volunteer work-style will determine what you do. However, you undoubtedly will perform certain key tasks. These are the kinds of activities that you will be doing:

Administering—the ministry team's programs, activities, meetings, minutes, materials, budget.

Facilitating—the ministry team's action proposals to the church council; your church's social involvement activities.

Researching—to find data on social issues; resource persons, agencies, materials; community needs; congregational attitudes, skills, and willingness to be involved.

Communicating—about social issues, educational events, community speakers, public meetings, positions of The United Methodist Church, actions of your annual conference and/or of the General Conference (every four years).

Educating—your congregation about the Social Principles and the General Conference positions on social issues (found in *The Book of Resolutions*); and about important justice issues in your community, state, and nation.

Acting—to carry out programs that the church council has assigned to the ministry team; to implement programs on a variety of issues on local, state, and national levels.

Witnessing—in your church and community about issues on which your congregation, annual conference, or General Conference has taken a stand.

Four Types of Congregational Involvement

The list of functions you might perform as ministry team chairperson of Church and Society suggests that you will point out different ways for your congregation to get involved in social issues. You will find that work on social issues falls into four broad categories: social service, social education, social witness, and social action.

These options for social involvement, used together, form a comprehensive effort to deal with a social issue. Each option supports the other, although you might use only one at a time. Consider the issue of hunger:

Social Service
Setting up a soup kitchen or providing a food pantry in your church or community is performing a social service. It makes an effort to meet and alleviate immediate human need.

Social Education
When your ministry team places stories about hunger in the local news media, church newsletter, church school classes, worship bulletin inserts, or other avenues, you are teaching your congregation and community about this issue, and carrying out social education. Social education provides a base for social service, witness, and action; sometimes it provides the spark for motivating others to action.

The General Board of Church and Society has many resources available to help in setting up and facilitating your ministry of social action. A short listing of those resources is at the back of this booklet. You can also visit the Web site at www.umc-gbcs.org for a complete list of all the materials, or call 202-488-5618.

Social Witness
Social witness says, "Here we stand." When your church makes public through a statement to the press, for example, its commitment with an action plan to eliminate hunger in your community (through social service, action, and education), it performs social witness. Fasting, taking part in demonstrations, boycotting certain businesses, prayer vigils—these are all forms of social witness.

Social Action

If your ministry team launches a letter-writing campaign or gives issue-related testimony to the County Board of Supervisors, it is performing a social action. Attempting to influence the decision-making process (through social service, education, and/or witness) is to engage in social action. You are seeking long-term social change in the problem's root causes. *You are seeking justice.*

Carrying Out a Comprehensive Ministry

Remember: these four categories are a rough checklist for carrying out a comprehensive ministry on a social issue. As you lead the ministry team's efforts, do not limit your ministry to one particular category. In fact, other ministry teams—for example, United Methodist Women, the United Methodist Men, the missions committee, or the committee on religion and race—may also be working on social issues. Therefore, you need to communicate regularly with the chairpersons of other ministry teams.

If you only operate a soup kitchen, for example, you may never deal with the root causes of hunger. You may, in fact, provide what some have called a "maintenance ministry" instead of a "prophetic ministry" that brings about real change.

Social involvement is identifying the need and then doing something about it. It is Christian love in action.

Jesus Got into Trouble

Serving, educating, witnessing, acting—these involvements on social issues frequently generate controversy. People disagree, sometimes strongly, on the ways to deal with social issues. Some United Methodists disagree with the positions their General Conference has adopted (see the Social Principles and the resolutions in the *Book of Resolutions 2004*).

United Methodists, like all people, have differing backgrounds and experiences that shape strongly held attitudes and values. Therefore, you will undoubtedly have to deal with some disagreements—even conflicts—but you will be following significant footsteps.

"Jesus got into trouble—and so will we—for attempting to transform society rather than to conform to it," noted the late George H. Outen, a former general secretary of the General Board of Church and Society. "But if we name the Name, and if we are followers of The Way, we are called to engage in the redemption of the social order. We are to help bring healing and wholeness to a broken world."

As the Church and Society leader, you will need to recognize and deal with conflict. You will need to be objective and nonjudgmental, to have accurate and complete information, to be fair but firm. Remember, conflict does not have to be destructive in your congregation. In a climate of mutual respect and openness, in which you are seeking to discern God's will and to be faithful people of God, both personal and group change can—and does—happen. Remember also that every church needs somone who is willing to "stir things up." Enjoy the ministry that you do. Try not to become overwhelmed by the issues. There are committed people in your congregation willing to help; don't be afraid to use their knowledge and skills.

Leadership Hints

Agreeing to disagree is important to achieving a climate of respect and openness. As you carry out your role as Church and Society leader, consider these steps toward strong leadership:

Never assume anything. Make reasonable preparation.

Bring everyone working with you to the same starting place.
Work to make everyone feel included; check to see that everyone understands all the language used in your meetings; and seek to bridge the gap between experienced and newer members of your ministry team.

Develop the ground rules together.
Help everyone understand her or his role; clarify minute-taking, procedures in your meetings, and follow-through expectations.

Follow problem-solving steps.
Identify the problem, hoped-for changes, necessary actions, and persons who have the authority to deal with the problem. Analyze the problem to determine gains from solutions and possible alternatives. Act to obtain necessary approval and move to implement the action.

Consider carefully the abilities necessary for effective group leadership.
Summarize where the group is, listing important points of discussion and identifying what items the group has dealt with and what work it still has to do. Ask questions in a way that will lead the group in a useful direction. Be patient with the group when it needs to struggle with an issue. Delegate tasks so that everyone makes a contribution to the ministry of the team.

Be sure everyone in the Church and Society ministry team understands and can discuss the foundations for social involvement. (Review the four methods congregations can engage a social issue, found on pages 8 and 9, and see below).

Take time to study the United Methodist Social Principles and *The Book of Resolutions*.

Foundations for Social Involvement

John Wesley practiced and preached a four-pronged approach to Christian faith that includes social involvement. This approach has become known as the Wesley Quadrilateral. He applied Scripture, tradition, experience, and reason to his positions. Traditionally, The United Methodist Church uses Scripture not literally but as a Holy Spirit-inspired, instructive guide to becoming faithful. While Scripture is central to faithful action and decision making, it is also a resource for study and interpretation, tested by tradition, experience, and reason. Therefore, you also can test all the work you do as a Church and Society ministry team against the Wesley Quadrilateral.

Scripture

As part of the Body of Christ, we are called to "be strong in the Lord and in the strength of his power. Put on the whole armor of God, so that you may be able to stand against the wiles of the devil. For our struggle is not against enemies of blood and flesh, but against the rulers, against the authorities, against the cosmic powers of this present darkness, against the spiritual forces of evil in the heavenly places" (Ephesians 6:10-12).

> There are numerous biblical references to helping the poor, the outcast, and the orphan. Take a moment with your ministry team and list as many references here as you can find. Which one speaks most powerfully to you?

Through his letter to the church in Corinth, Paul tells the church universal that, as we work, we will be "afflicted in every way, but not crushed; perplexed, but not driven to despair; persecuted, but not forsaken; struck down, but not destroyed" (2 Corinthians 4:8-9).

The Gospel of Luke speaks of duties and sacrifices: "The Spirit of the Lord is upon me, because he has anointed me to bring good news to the poor. He has sent me to proclaim release to the captives and recovery of sight to the blind, to let the oppressed go free, to proclaim the year of the Lord's favor" (Luke 4:18–19).

Likewise, Matthew records Jesus' call to feed the hungry, clothe the naked, find shelter for the homeless, minister to the sick and the imprisoned, and welcome the stranger (Matthew 25:35-40). Matthew also teaches that our social action will sometimes create division. Jesus says, "Do not think that I have come to bring peace to the earth; I have not come to bring peace, but a sword. For I have come to set a man against his father, and a daughter against her mother" (Matthew 10:34-35).

Dietrich Bonhoeffer, in *The Cost of Discipleship,* notes that Luke speaks of the joy of preaching forgiveness while requiring repentance, and of the grace of God reflected in social action. The "Song of Mary" expresses this joy and grace: "My soul magnifies the Lord, and my spirit rejoices in God my Savior.... He has shown strength with his arm; he has scattered the proud in the thoughts of their hearts. He has brought down the powerful from their thrones, and lifted up the lowly; he has filled the hungry with good things, and sent the rich away empty" (Luke 1:46-53).

As Bishop Kenneth L. Carder has written in his book *Sermons on United Methodist Beliefs,* "The Bible remains the primary tool we use to approach the thorny issues of our time." Carder suggests that as we work on today's issues, this sacred tool provides a foundation of truth—in Creation stories showing the interrelatedness of all the earth, in the prophets' calls for justice, in Jesus' love for all humanity, in Paul's letters instructing the churches, and in the vision of God's *shalom* calling us to act to insure justice for all people.

Tradition

Since the days when John Wesley declared that the world was his parish, Methodists have put into action his belief that "one cannot minister by proxy." Members of The United Methodist Church have often taken forthright positions on controversial issues involving Christian principles.

For instance, early members of the Methodist Church and the Evangelical United Brethren Church (EUB) expressed their opposition to slavery, to smuggling, and to cruel treatment of prisoners.

In 1908, the Methodist Episcopal Church (North) adopted a social creed. Within the next decade similar statements were adopted by the Methodist Episcopal Church, South, and by the Methodist Protestant Church. The EUB Church adopted a statement of social principles in 1946, when the Church of the United Brethren in Christ and the Evangelical Church united.

In 1972, four years after the 1968 union of the EUB Church and Methodist Church, the General Conference of The United Methodist Church adopted a new statement of Social Principles, which has been slightly revised by successive General Conferences every four years since.

The Preface of the Social Principles provides a succinct description of the purpose of this important document:

The Social Principles are a prayerful and thoughtful effort on the part of the General Conference to speak to the human issues in the contemporary world from a sound biblical and theological foundation as historically demonstrated in United Methodist traditions. They are intended to be instructive and persuasive in the best of the prophetic spirit. The Social Principles are a call to all members of The United Methodist Church to a prayerful, studied dialogue of faith and practice.

In addition, the United Methodist General Conference passes resolutions that are published in *The Book of Resolutions*. The Social Principles and the resolutions form the foundation for United Methodist involvement in social issues.

The *2004 Book of Discipline* and *The Book of Resolutions* are available from The United Methodist Publishing House. Call 1-800-672-1789.

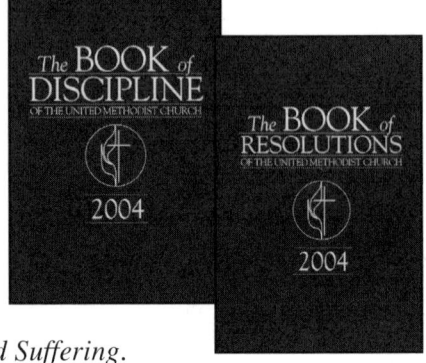

Reason

"If Christ's life was not political, then what was it?" asks South African Anglican Archbishop Desmond Tutu in his book *Hope and Suffering*. Members of the Body of Christ are called to reflect on the meaning of social justice and its implications for our involvement in social justice ministry.

Justice, says social ethicist Walter Brueggemann, is finding out what belongs to whom and giving it back to them.

"So do not lightly read of Jesus' intention to bring good news to the poor by failing to think about what is good news to a poor person," said George Outen. "Let the church not gloss over the upheavals caused by releasing the captives and liberating the oppressed. Things are never the same when the blind receive their sight and the brokenhearted are healed."

As *The Book of Discipline* states so clearly (¶104):

> *By reason we read and interpret Scripture.*
> *By reason we determine whether our Christian witness is clear.*
> *By reason we ask questions of faith and seek to understand God's action and will.*
> *By reason we organize the understandings that compose our witness and render them internally coherent.*

> *By reason we test the congruence of our witness to the biblical testimony and to the traditions which mediate that testimony to us.*
> *By reason we relate our witness to the full range of human knowledge, experience, and service.*

Experience

The statement on "Our Theological Task" (¶104) in *The Book of Discipline* notes wisely:

> *Our experience interacts with Scripture. We read Scripture in light of the conditions and events that help shape who we are, and we interpret our experience in terms of Scripture. . . . Christian experience . . . confirms the biblical message for our present. It illumines our understanding of God and creation, and motivates us to make sensitive moral judgments.*
>
> *Although profoundly personal, Christian experience is also corporate; our theological task is informed by the experience of the Church and by the common experiences of all humanity. In our attempt to understand the biblical message, we recognize that God's gift of liberating love embraces the whole of creation.*

For example, many Christians are acting to oppose the continuing spread of legalized gambling. Their reading of Scripture reveals the biblical mandate to conserve the resources and gifts, including money, that God has granted us. The United Methodist Church, from its earliest days, has traditionally opposed gambling as an evil "menace to society" and to individuals. The church's objection is based on the destructive nature of seeking material gain by chance and at the expense of a neighbor.

The church's experience, as well as the experience of individuals, reveals that greed impoverishes persons who seek to obtain "something for nothing," contributes to the breakdown of families and communities, and even erodes good government.

Combine all the above, and it is clear why The United Methodist Church, along with many other faith communities, has opposed gambling.

Scripture, tradition, reason, and experience should move every Church and Society ministry team and for that matter every concerned Christian into efforts to protect the basic human rights and dignity of all persons, and to uplift people who are poor and exploited.

Getting Started

Of all the steps you will be taking as a Church and Society chairperson, and as a ministry team, getting started will be the most important. These first steps will largely determine the effects of what you do. Here are some suggestions for getting started:

- Read carefully the description of your responsibilities in *The Book of Discipline*.
- Study these Guidelines. You might also look through or read the Guidelines for other ministry teams. These may give you ideas for building relationships with people in these areas as you work on social concerns.
- Study and discuss the art illustrating these Guidelines. Consider whether any of it represents issues needing work in your community.
- Talk over your assignment with your pastor, your predecessor Church and Society ministry team chairperson, the chairperson of your church council, and others in the congregation who you know are involved in social issues.
- Read "Our Common Mission" on page ___ of this booklet as a foundation for your work with your congregation.
- Try to find at least two or three other persons to work with you. If a Church and Society ministry team was not named by the nominations committee, make a list of others in your congregation whom you might involve.
- Know who is on the team. Ask yourself:
    1. What gifts do they bring to the ministry team?
    2. What concerns and interests do they have regarding justice ministries?
    3. How well can we work together? (You might want to try a few "team building" exercises to bring out some of the strengths and areas for growth of your group.)
    4. Is this a one-issue group, or do the ministry team members have diverse interests, representing a cross section of your congregation?

- Be prepared to share with clarity the nature and purpose of the Church and Society ministry team.
- Talk with other ministry team chairpersons and coordinators about program needs and possibilities; discuss ways to work cooperatively.
- Get acquainted with the structure of your local church and determine your relationships to other groups. Think about what other groups you might enlist as coworkers on various issues. Much of what you might plan to do with the congregation might be done through other program groups. For example, for the church school, you might suggest a class on the Social

Principles. Your ministry team could help coordinate a study about a justice issue—such as homelessness, hunger, or drug abuse—with United Methodist Women or Men. For youth groups, you might suggest community service projects implementing environmental concerns. In short, *your congregation becomes an extension of your Church and Society ministry team.*

- Survey your congregation to determine members' current involvement with social issues and to solicit their suggestions for church action. Enable members to have some ownership in what the Church and Society ministry team does. Ask repeatedly:
    1. Do the issues on which we are working really affect society and future generations?
    2. What are the local, national, and international ramifications of issues such as hunger, drug and alcohol abuse, and the arms race?
    3. What can our church do at one (or perhaps all) of these levels?
- Get the congregation involved early. Share with members your enthusiasm about this ministry—in the newsletter, bulletin reminders, and announcements.
- Know who your partners are:
    1. Contact the district director of Church and Society and the chairperson of the conference Board of Church and Society to learn more about resources and possible training experiences.
    2. Contact the conference Council on Ministries and talk with the staff person responsible for Church and Society matters.
    3. Call or write to the Communications unit of the General Board of Church and Society to ask for program and resource suggestions (202-488-5600). Also, make use of the GBCS Web site, at www.umc-gbcs.org.
    4. Contact local and state councils or churches and other social involvement groups, such as the League of Women Voters, agencies dealing with drug abuse, a suicide hot-line and prevention group, or a facility for the homeless, and discuss ways your church can get involved.
- Know your local community. Ask yourself:
    1. What is happening in our community?
    2. What are the issues in our community—poverty, homelessness, drugs, suicide, gambling, housing, education?
    3. What are the strengths and weaknesses of the community?
    4. What groups are already involved in social justice issues, in the congregation and larger community? How can we join with them?
- Consider ways to get information from community, state, and nation.:
    1. Interviewing the mayor, police chief, city council members, school administrators, directors of community agencies, executives of councils of churches, and other persons in positions of authority.

2. Meeting and talking with welfare recipients, migrant workers, aged persons, people who are homeless or live in low-income housing.
3. Monitoring sessions of your city government and its various agencies.
4. Regularly reading local newspapers and magazines, listening to radio, and watching television documentaries.

- Begin to develop, for a proposal to your church council, some realistic goals for social involvement by your church. Consider a program of education about community issues on which your church might provide some witness, develop a service project, and/or take action.
- Recommend dates for the church calendar—for example, Human Relations Day (on the Sunday before the observance of Martin Luther King's birthday), Peace-with-Justice Sunday (the Sunday after Pentecost), or UN Week (the week before the October 24th anniversary date of the founding of the United Nations).
- Know what you will do and when you will do it—commonly known as "setting priorities." Envision what you and the members of your ministry team hope to accomplish. Consider these important questions in this quest for a vision:
    1. Where would we like to be a year (or two or five) from now?
    2. What goals (markers on the way toward the vision) would we like to have accomplished? (A goal could be simply stated: "By 2007, First UMC will be a barrier-free church building.")
    3. What does the vision look like?

Suppose you envision a well-informed congregation, understanding social justice ministries, willing to share in that ministry, and supporting the work of the Church and Society ministry team. With this vision, you will then need to ask:
1. What will it take to move toward our vision?
2. What will have to happen first?
3. What are the second, third, fourth steps?
4. Who will do what?
5. When will each step be accomplished?
6. What resources do we need?
7. Is it do-able?

Once you are answering these questions, you are underway. Put down the steps on paper and begin to move toward your vision

STATED VISION:

Who?　　　　　When?　　　　　What?

1. _____

2. _____

3. _____

4. _____

5. _____

Cultivating Relationships

As you carry out your ministry-team responsibilities, you will naturally develop relationships.

- inside your local church;
- with persons in the various levels in The United Methodist Church;
- with ecumenical or coalition groups in your community;
- and with some persons or groups most isolated from society.

Within Your Congregation

The groups you will work with include:

The Council on Ministries. They must approve all your ministry team's program proposals. You are the council's chief advisor on critical social issues.

The Church Council, Administrative Board, or Administrative Council. They must approve funding proposals for particular programs sponsored by your ministry team. Here you participate in the policymaking and financial decisions of your church.

Age-level and family coordinators. These can help you work with and coordinate programs for specific age levels.

The Pastor and other church staff. These should be aware of and work with you in all your efforts. The pastor often receives mailings from the conference office and from general church agencies that relate to your ministry.

Other ministry teams. These can help you work with and coordinate social concerns programs related to Christian unity and interreligious concerns, education, evangelism, higher education and campus ministry, missions, religion and race, the status and role of women, stewardship, trustees, and worship.

In addition, many churches have a person who is focused on health and welfare ministries and shares the concern for adequate health care for all persons. A communications coordinator may handle necessary communication tasks, such as publicity, and provide information regarding printed and audiovisual resources (obtained through your conference media center).

As you discover your community needs and begin to respond to them, you may find that other ministry teams in your congregation (or from other congregations, the district, or annual conference) are addressing the same problem, perhaps from a different perspective. These common concerns provide the basis for a relationship between two or more ministry teams, strengthening your social justice witness.

Where common concerns do not occur naturally, be creative in finding ways to work together. For example, think about actions on drug and alcohol concerns that could involve all the ministry teams of the church.

Within The United Methodist Connection

You will probably be in contact with individuals and groups at other levels of The United Methodist Church:

District Director of Church and Society. This person works with the district Council on Ministries, and should communicate regularly with your congregation (possibly the pastor) to share information on new resources, training, programs, and/or problems and issues going on in the district and beyond. You can take the initiative to contact the district director by calling your district office (ask your pastor or church secretary for the number). Give the district director information about the needs of your church or community, or suggest programs you would like to see developed at the district or conference levels.

Annual conference Board of Church and Society. This Board serves as the key link between district directors, local churches, and the General Board of Church and Society. Each annual conference has a Board of Church and Society—or equivalent structure—responsible for addressing social concerns particularly relevant to that area. Your pastor should have information about your conference board, its chairperson and other officers, and issues on which it is working. The information is also available in your annual conference journal.

Annual conference staff person related to Church and Society. This person relates to the conference Board of Church and Society, district directors and/or district committees, and the General Board of Church and Society. Find out who this staff person is and call him or her to get help or make suggestions. Also, find out if your annual conference offers training opportunities during the year.

General Board of Church and Society (GBCS). This Board seeks to influence, from the perspective of the Christian faith and the stances of The United Methodist Church, national public policy. One of the four national program boards of your denomination, the GBCS develops and carries out the general church's program on social issues.

Its board members are elected from across the entire Church. Staff members research and interpret legislation, then communicate with, educate, and assist in training other United Methodists about social issues and legislation.

The GBCS staff operates from offices at the United Methodist Building on Capitol Hill (100 Maryland Ave., NE, Washington, D.C., 20002; 202/488-5600). The GBCS also has an office at the Church Center for the United Nations in New York City, located across the street from the UN (at 777 United Nations Plaza, New York, NY 10017; 212/682-3633). This office is staffed cooperatively with the Women's Division of the General Board of Global Ministries.

For your work on social issues, the GBCS produces helpful resources. (See "Resources" at the end of this booklet. A complete listing of GBCS resources is carried in a catalog available from the GBCS Service Department, and also on the GBCS Web site, at www.umc-gbcs.org. You will also find a toll-free number listed there, along with the legislative hotline and updates for action alerts on national legislative efforts.

Coalitions

Formed by a variety of distinct groups with a common purpose, coalitions can tackle major tasks collectively, therefore more effectively. By pooling their limited financial resources, member groups can support a sizable coalition. Furthermore, coalitions needing additional funds for a particular project or program frequently expand their resources by enlisting the support of individuals and foundations.

Coalitions do not speak in the name of their constituent groups but work in their behalf. They can be expanded, contracted, or ended to meet changing needs.

If your ministry team wants to organize a coalition to deal with a particular issue, try to find help from someone who has had experience in community organizing. Then contact those persons or groups who have expressed interest in coming together to work on the issue. Your church's needs might be better served, however, by participation in existing organizations. For a detailed listing of the national coalitions in which the GBCS participates, write to: Assistant General Secretary, Resourcing Congregational Life, GBCS, 100 Maryland Ave., NE, Washington, D.C. 20002.

Ecumenical and Interfaith Groups

Within Christianity, the varied traditions, doctrines, and experiences of differing churches and denominations can be drawn together in one organization for the enrichment of the members. These ecumenical groups are actually coalitions in which the members work together toward common goals—including Christian unity.

The National Council of Churches of Christ is perhaps the most well-known example of an ecumenical organization. At the local level, churches have frequently come together to battle legalized gambling or to work on drug concerns.

In the same way, interfaith groups, such as the National Conference of Christians and Jews, often help churches and denominations gain broader insights into social issues.

Ministry With Those Who Are Marginalized

"The Social Community" section of the Social Principles (found in part 3 of *The Book of Discipline* or at the beginning of *The Book of Resolutions*) discusses the rights of various groups frequently alienated or left out of mainstream society.

Think about these groups in your own community, area, or country: racial and ethnic groups, religious minorities, children, youth, the aged, single women heads of households, persons with disabilities, persons addicted to drugs, alcohol, or gambling, ex-offenders, persons who are ill, or persons of homosexual orientation.

Your Church and Society ministry team should focus attention on the concerns of persons and groups most marginalized within the society. Your social involvement needs to be on behalf of, and in cooperation with, people who are most frequently isolated, needing to mobilize their power, or used as scapegoats for problems in society. Matthew 25:40 reports Jesus' stance: "Just as you did it to one of the least of these who are members of my family, you did it to me."

You need to understand, empathize with, and work with a wide variety of people. Use these questions as a starting point:
- How are they isolated?
- What are their needs?
- What groups are working for, or with, them?
- What might our church do to help them?
- How can we make contact with these groups or people?

Checklist for Planning and Action

The following questions are designed to help you and your ministry team plan for action when addressing a social issue. The list is not exhaustive; you and your team will think of other questions as you undergo your ministry together. Keep track of the questions and answers in a notebook or file folder as a way to help your ministry team improve its witness to the church and society.

Consider Issues/Needs

Gather information on a variety of issues or needs in your community. A survey of your congregation and an analysis of the community are good places to start.
- Determine which issue (or perhaps more than one) is most important; in other words, set a priority list.
- Find out more about the issue or problem:
    1. What is the problem?
    2. What are the causes?
    3. Where and when is this an issue?
    4. Who has information about this issue?
    5. What change needs to happen?
    6. Why should the Church and Society ministry team (and other members of the congregation) be involved in this issue?
    7. What other ministry team in your congregation/district/annual conference can help? For example, seek out people from Religion and Race to deal with issues concerning racism; The General Commission on the Status and Role of Women (COSROW), or Women's Division of The General Board of Global Ministries, can help with women's issues. There are numerous other boards and agencies—with district or annual conference organizations—that can help.
    8. What type of social involvement might your congregation carry out in relation to this problem?

Develop Strategies
- Set learning/action goals for dealing with the issue.
- List the positive forces that will help achieve these goals.
- List the negative forces that will inhibit reaching the goals.
- Take actions to lessen the negative forces and strengthen the positive.
- Read about and study the issue.

- Connect with other ministry teams working on social issues.
- Interview persons affected by the issue as well as decision makers who affect the issue.
- Attend meetings and observe critical sessions of public groups.
- Decide who will do what on the issue.
- Consider carefully how to make the best use of resources. Answer these questions:
    1. What are the gaps—in education, witness, action—on this particular issue?
    2. What resources—human, financial—will our church bring to this effort?
    3. How much money will we need to put this plan into action?
    4. How many other groups are, or will be, working on this issue? How can we work with them in a coordinated fashion?
    5. What agencies are advocates for those who are poor?
    6. Will our resources make a difference in the outcome?
    7. Does our congregation have enough resources to do the job?
    8. Can our congregation develop the vision to inspire, motivate, and sustain a number of members' involvement in the issue?

Get Approval, Act, Review

- Take your plans for dealing with the issue to the church's Council on Ministries (or church council). There, the plan will be reviewed, discussed, coordinated, and (hopefully!) approved.
- Seek adequate funding to carry out the planned actions.
- Determine who will implement the action if it is taken by a group other than the Church and Society ministry team.
- When your plans go to the church council, attend the meeting to support the proposal.
- Do your homework.
- Be prepared to answer questions, particularly if the proposal deal with a controversial issue.
- Get to work!
- And last but not least, evaluate, evaluate, evaluate.

Resources

You can find a wide variety of helpful resources in your own area. Don't overlook the local media—newspapers, radio stations, television stations, magazines, journalists—as well as local libraries, universities, think tanks, community leaders, other agencies, and other churches. In addition to your first resource, the Bible, the following resources will provide you necessary information and a foundation for your ministry.

The Social Principles
The overarching statement of United Methodist positions approved by General Conference on a wide range of social issues, the Social Principles statement is available in three formats:

1. *The Book of Discipline, 2004.* (*The Book of Discipline* is the book of church law and covenant for The United Methodist Church);
2. *The Book of Resolutions, 2004;*
3. A booklet containing the Social Principles, available in English, Spanish, and Korean, from the Service Department of the General Board of Church and Society, 100 Maryland Ave., NE, Washington, D.C. 20002. A study/leader's guide is also available. You may want to order enough copies for your entire congregation.

The first two books (which your pastor should have in her or his library) and the English booklet of the Social Principles are available from your nearest Cokesbury store (1-800-672-1789).

A videotape program interpreting the Social Principles for adults, *More Than Words,* and another for confirmation-aged youth, *The Retreat,* are both available from the GBCS Service Department.

The Book of Resolutions, 2004
Published by The United Methodist Publishing House, with editorial assistance from staff members of the General Board of Church and Society, *The Book of Resolutions* is the denomination's best kept secret, and includes all currently valid resolutions adopted by General Conference. It also includes a user's guide. Contact Cokesbury to purchase a copy.

Faithful Witness on Today's Issues Booklets
Produced by the General Board of Church and Society, each booklet in this series contains selected current valid General Conference resolutions on one topic, such as drug and alcohol concerns, peace, or housing. Each includes

related statements from the Social Principles and brief study/discussion material. These booklets are available from the GBCS Service Department.

Christian Social Action Magazine

Published by the General Board of Church and Society, this magazine includes information on and analysis of social issues from the perspective of the Christian faith and the positions of The United Methodist Church. "CSA is excellent," wrote one reader. "I encourage anyone interested in social issues to read it."

The magazine includes the eight-page "Word from Washington" newsletter, which discusses Church and Society programs, activities, and resources. The magazine occasionally focuses entirely on one issue, such as gambling, human rights, genetic engineering, or agriculture. These special issues are then available to congregations as study resources.

To subscribe or obtain more information, or to get a sample copy, write to: *Christian Social Action,* Circulation Department, 100 Maryland Ave., NE, Washington, D.C. 20002; or phone 202-488-5616. You can also visit CSA on the Web at www.umc-gbcs.org.

The Worldwide Web

The General Board of Church and Society has its presence on the Web at <www.umc-gbcs.org>. There you can keep up to date instantly with Action Alerts and Press Statements of the Board, as well as information on a variety of social issues. Staff names, phone numbers, and e-mail addresses may also be looked up. The site also provides opportunity for you to dialogue with staff, as well as links to several other social justice ministry Web pages.

Resource Catalogs

To obtain your free catalog of Church and Society materials from the GBCS, contact the Service Department at: 100 Maryland Ave., NE, Washington, D.C., 20002; phone 202-488-5618. The resource catalog is also available on the GBCS Web site www.umc-gbcs.org. The GBCS Legislative Hotline provides weekly updates on legislation before Congress. The Hotline is available 24 hours a day at 1-800-455-2645.

Register of Citizen Opinion

This is a directory of Congress, produced annually by the General Board of Church and Society. It includes a guide to political action, lists of members of Congress and their committee assignments, members of the cabinet and Supreme Court justices, phone numbers of governmental agencies, and lists of political action resource agencies and resources. This information-packed booklet is available from GBCS Service Department.

The Interpreter Magazine

Several copies of the program journal of The United Methodist Church are sent free to each local church; check with your pastor to see whether you can receive one of those. If not, at least make sure that you get to see *The Interpreter* when it arrives. Most issues have an "Idea Mart" Church and Society column with information for your ministry team. The magazine also carries descriptions of new resources, feature articles dealing with social issues, and information on special-day resources.

United Methodist Seminars on National and International Affairs

The seminar program at GBCS offer opportunities for your ministry team, your local church, your church youth group, and many other groups, to study national and international justice issues. Each seminar is tailor-made for each group.

Groups from all over the denomination travel annually to the United Methodist Building across the street from the U.S. Capitol in Washington, D.C., or to the Church Center for the United Nations, across the street from the headquarters of the international organization. In these settings, seminar participants study the causes of injustice in the world and examine the involvement of the United States and other nations. The seminar program also sponsors trips outside the United States to study the social justice issues of various cultures and communities.

The seminar program is sponsored and funded (in New York City) by the Women's Division of the General Board of Global Ministries, and (in Washington, D.C.) by the General Board of Church and Society. Seminar designers staff the programs in both locations. For information on seminar topics, contact:

Seminar Program, General Board of Church and Society, 100 Maryland Ave., NE, Washington, D.C., 20002; 202-488-5611, or visit their Web site at www.umc-gbcs.org.

Seminar Program, Church Center for the United Nations, 777 United Nations Plaza, New York, NY, 10017; 212-682-3633.